ANGOLA: HUMAN RIGHTS

EXECUTIVE SUMMARY

Angola is a constitutional republic. The ruling Popular Movement for the Liberation of Angola (MPLA), led by President Jose Eduardo dos Santos, has been in power since independence in 1975. The MPLA exercised tight, centralized control over government planning, policymaking, and media outlets. In August 2012 the government held the first fully constituted presidential and legislative elections in the country's history. The MPLA won 71.8 percent of the vote, and in September 2012 dos Santos began a five-year term as president. Domestic and international observers reported that polling throughout the country was peaceful and largely well organized. Observers highlighted problems associated with the ruling party's control of media and other resources, the inability of many citizens to vote because of confusion about their registration status, and insufficient credentials for domestic and political party election observers. Authorities generally maintained effective control over the security forces. Security forces committed human rights abuses.

The three most important human rights abuses were cruel, excessive, and degrading punishment, including reported cases of torture and beatings as well as unlawful killings by police and other security personnel; limits on freedoms of assembly, association, speech, and press; and official corruption and impunity.

Other human rights abuses included: arbitrary or unlawful deprivation of life; harsh and potentially life-threatening prison conditions; arbitrary arrest and detention; lengthy pretrial detention; impunity for human rights abusers; lack of due process and judicial inefficiency; infringements on citizens' privacy rights and forced evictions without compensation; restrictions on nongovernmental organizations (NGOs); discrimination and violence against women; abuse of children; trafficking in persons; limits on workers' rights; and forced labor.

The government took limited steps to prosecute or punish officials who committed abuses; however, accountability was weak due to a lack of checks and balances, lack of institutional capacity, a culture of impunity, and widespread government corruption.

Section 1. Respect for the Integrity of the Person, Including Freedom from:

a. Arbitrary or Unlawful Deprivation of Life

There were reports the government or its agents committed arbitrary or unlawful killings, including politically motivated killings. Political parties, human rights activists, and domestic media sources reported that political party supporters and security forces arbitrarily killed at least 12 persons during the year.

For example, on March 30, police in Luanda allegedly killed a man by shooting him twice in the head after he confronted them about beating one of his friends, reportedly over suspicions that the friend had tried to steal cigarettes from a street vendor. The family of the deceased attempted to press charges, but authorities took no known action.

On November 22, presidential guards shot Manuel Hilberto "Ganga" de Carvalho, a member of the second largest opposition party Broad Convergence for the Salvation of Angola, Electoral Coalition (CASA-CE), when he tried to flee following his detention for placing posters in an allegedly restricted area. Ganga later died in a hospital.

Media reported fights between supporters of the two main political parties, the ruling MPLA and opposition National Union for the Total Independence of Angola (UNITA). On May 10, MPLA supporters used sticks, clubs, and machetes to destroy a UNITA convention area. UNITA supporters then initiated a fight with the MPLA group, which had wrecked their stage. Several hours later, a smaller group of MPLA supporters went to the house of a UNITA party secretary, and when one of his colleagues went outside to confront them, they allegedly beat him to death with rocks and sticks. Police did not arrest any of the alleged attackers.

A prominent human rights activist reported the private security firm Bicuar killed an artisanal miner in the diamond-rich region of Lunda Norte on April 20. The police detained seven Bicuar guards and released five of them after questioning. It was not known if any action was taken against the two remaining guards.

Police conducted an investigation into the execution-style killing of seven unarmed civilians in December 2012 in the Cacuaco neighborhood of Luanda. A prominent human rights organization claimed that police themselves were behind the killings. A police report claimed only one man had been killed, he was a known thief, and a motorist shot him during a botched carjacking. Despite the widely divergent versions of the event, police considered the case closed.

Impunity remained a serious problem, and police seldom released the results of investigations into security force abuses.

Land mines placed during the civil war and other explosive remnants of war (ERW) remained a threat. The National Inter-Ministerial Commission for Demining and Humanitarian Assistance (CNIDAH) compiled nationwide statistics on mine victims. As of September CNIDAH had registered nine fatalities, 17 injuries, and one vehicle destroyed due to mine incidents, a slight decrease compared with 2012. According to the National Institute for Demining Affairs, most recent incidents were related to ERW rather than land mines and were frequently detonated by children, who found the design appealing, or by adults, who erroneously believed the explosives contained marketable materials. The government continued to strengthen and expand national demining capacity during the year, and it partnered extensively with international and domestic NGOs on demining operations and mine-risk education.

b. Disappearance

Unlike the previous year, there were no credible reports of politically motivated disappearances.

The cases of Alves Kamulingue and Isaias Kassule, who disappeared in May 2012, continued to draw significant attention throughout the year. Several domestic and international civil society organizations demanded that the government admit to having abducted and killed the two men. During her April visit, the UN High Commissioner for Human Rights (UNHCHR), Navi Pillay, raised this case with the minister of interior and the attorney general, and they assured her that an investigation was ongoing. In November the attorney general announced police had detained four individuals, three of whom were reportedly officers from the National Institute for Criminal Investigations (DNIC) and one of whom was a member of the State Intelligence and Security Services (SINSE); the four men reportedly had admitted to the crime. The investigation was ongoing at year's end, and no sentencing had taken place.

On March 27, police detained Alberto dos Santos because of his alleged involvement in the disappearance of Alves Kamulingue and Isaias Kassule. Dos Santos reportedly witnessed the kidnapping in May 2012 and had been waiting almost a year for police to interview him. Instead of questioning him, however, police reportedly detained him under the suspicion that he was complicit in the kidnapping. Several civil society groups believe police detained him because he might be able to provide evidence to prove that elements of the government were behind the politically motivated kidnapping. Police released dos Santos in early October, more than six months after originally detaining him, with no formal charges against him.

c. Torture and Other Cruel, Inhuman, or Degrading Treatment or Punishment

Government security forces reportedly tortured, beat, and otherwise abused persons. Reports of beatings and other abuses en route to and in police stations during interrogations remained common.

In June a member of a youth movement claimed that police tortured him after taking him into custody because he participated in an antigovernment protest. According to the man's mother, police used pliers to rip a fingernail from his hand, gave him a black eye, and covered his body with bruises from severe beatings. It was unknown if police took any action to investigate the claims of abuse.

On September 20, police detained without charge and physically abused journalists Rafael Marques, Alexandre Neto, and Coque Mukuta for over four hours. Reportedly, police stomped on the detainees, beat them with batons, and threatened to kill them (see sections 2.a. and 2.d.).

The government rarely held accountable police and other security forces for torture reportedly committed in previous years. Although the government punished some violators administratively, few prosecutions were known to have occurred during the year. Police were not, however, able to act with complete impunity. On two separate occasions, videos surfaced showing prison guards beating prisoners. Although the incidents took place in 2012, the ministry of interior initiated an investigation in both cases shortly after the videos became public. In the first case, authorities fired several guards and prison officials or otherwise punished them administratively. The ministry reportedly suspended at least 16 guards, firemen, and other officials in the second case, although it was unknown if they faced criminal charges. The government's swift reaction to these alleged incidents of prisoner abuse reportedly appeared to be a reaction to public outcry and not to an independent accountability mechanism. Other cases of similar abuse reportedly occurred and went unpunished.

The government continued to conduct operations to identify, detain, and expel irregular immigrants. In Luanda border control agents focused on irregular migrants from West Africa and certain Asian countries (including China and Vietnam). Border control agents placed emphasis on operations in the provinces bordering the Democratic Republic of the Congo (DRC): Cabinda, Zaire, Uige, Malange, Lunda Norte, Lunda Sul, and Moxico. In particular, in diamond-rich Lunda Norte Province, NGOs and the media reported acts of violence and degrading treatment, including rape and sexual abuse, associated with these operations. In April UNHCHR Pillay visited a border crossing in Lunda Norte and stated sexual abuse of female migrants and property theft continued to be problems. The government did not carry out thorough and impartial investigations into past allegations of serious abuse of migrants by its security forces during expulsions from the country, continued to deny the veracity of the allegations, and failed to prosecute alleged perpetrators.

There was one known report of abuse by the army. In March the family of an officer-in-training claimed he was raped by his commanding officer. The rape led to internal bleeding and a prolapsed rectum, which after going undertreated, led to the victim's death. No known action was taken against the offending officer.

A prominent human rights activist reported abuses by private security companies hired by diamond companies in Lunda Norte, noting these companies routinely killed and tortured miners in the province. He also reported regular complaints of sexual abuse of women.

Portuguese prosecutors dismissed a defamation case against Rafael Marques in February in which nine generals and two private security companies alleged that Marques had slandered them in his 2011 book *Blood Diamonds: Corruption and Torture in Angola*. The generals and security companies decided to press their defamation case and officially opened a suit against him in July. The case was underway at year's end.

Prison and Detention Center Conditions

Prison conditions were potentially harsh and life threatening, and domestic NGOs and media continued to highlight corruption, overcrowding, and deaths possibly resulting from poor conditions. A 2012 Human Rights Watch (HRW) report found that prison guards committed abuses, including sexual violence, torture, and inhumane treatment of migrants, often acting with the complicity of different security services.

Physical Conditions: In September Vice Minister of Interior for Correctional Services Jose Bamoquina Lau said there were approximately 11,000 convicted criminals in the country, 8,000 pretrial detainees, and 400 persons "preventively detained" because of past criminal behavior. Lau acknowledged that overcrowding remained a major problem in the state's 34 prisons.

The vast majority of prisoners and detainees were between 18 and 31 years of age, with nearly half being under 21. The ministry oversaw one all-female prison, which held approximately 700 prisoners and detainees. No information was available about the number of juveniles in state custody.

According to the ministry of interior, authorities did not hold men, women, and juveniles together in prisons.

Children under three years of age may stay with their mothers in prison but may also leave the prison with family members. The ministry of interior worked with social assistants to ensure the children's wellbeing. The children were entitled to receive dietary supplements, milk, and diapers, and the women's prison had a day care center.

Provincial prisons reportedly housed juveniles, often incarcerated for petty theft, together with adults because separate juvenile detention centers and juvenile court systems did not exist. Luanda prisons separated juveniles from the main prison population. There was little coordination among government ministries to address the factors leading to juvenile crime.

Authorities frequently held pretrial detainees with sentenced inmates, and short-term detainees with those serving long-term sentences for violent crimes, especially in provincial prisons.

Prison conditions varied widely between urban and rural areas. Prisons generally provided some medical care, sanitation, potable water, and food, although it was customary for families to bring food to prisoners. The ministry of interior claimed to spend approximately 2,850 kwanzas ($30) per inmate per day to provide food and services, although some observers doubted the figure was that high. A prison hospital in Luanda serviced prisoners throughout the country with serious medical conditions. The hospital had more than 100 beds, 10 doctors, and 10 nurses.

Nine prisoners were killed and at least 22 injured in a Luanda prison in December. The prisoners reportedly belonged to rival gangs and killed and injured each other in a large riot.

Authorities provided prisoners education to lessen recidivism and promote social reintegration. The ministry of justice and human rights continued its "New Direction, New Opportunities" program in partnership with the ministry of interior. The program provides technical training and social education programs to help improve prisoners' reintegration into society. In some prisons inmates grew food and made bread to sell to police and on the local market, while in other prisons authorities allowed inmates to work in local factories. Limited vocational training was done in a public-private partnership with local industry. The labor was voluntary. In some prisons inmates had access to sports and recreation facilities.

Administration: The ministry of interior claimed it was taking steps to improve prison recordkeeping, and that efforts continued to transition from a manual recordkeeping system to a computerized database, including biometric data and a link to other agencies, such as police and justice. It claimed that adequate statistics were available in each facility, and that authorities were able to locate every prisoner.

The law provides the right for prisoners to practice their religion. The government allowed prisoners to submit complaints to judicial authorities without censorship and request investigation of conditions. The government investigated and monitored prison and detention center conditions.

Some offenders, including violent offenders, reportedly were able to pay fines and bribes to secure their freedom, but it was unclear how prevalent this practice was. There was no official policy regarding alternatives to incarceration for nonviolent offenders.

An independent office of the ombudsman existed to mediate between an aggrieved public, including prisoners, and an offending public office or institution. The office had no decision-making or adjudicative powers, but it helped citizens access justice and advised government entities on citizen rights. The office also published reports and educated the public about human rights and the role of the ombudsman.

Independent Monitoring: The government permitted visits to prisons by independent local and international human rights observers and foreign diplomats. The International Committee of the Red Cross visited the Cabinda prison and border detention centers in Lunda Norte Province. A spokesperson for a local NGO reported visiting a Luanda prison and described conditions as increasingly humane, although overcrowding remained a serious concern. The ministry of interior claimed it invites members of the diplomatic corps to visit a prison every year.

Improvements: The ministry of interior built a new prison in Huambo Province in 2012, and had new prisons under construction in Uige, Luanda, Malange, Namibe, Cunene, and Lunda Sul provinces.

Authorities completed the construction of a juvenile detention center in Kwanza Sul Province during the year.

d. Arbitrary Arrest or Detention

The law prohibits arbitrary arrest and detention; however, security forces often did not respect these prohibitions.

According to several NGO and civil society sources, police arbitrarily arrested individuals without due process and routinely detained individuals who participated in antigovernment protests, despite this right being protected by the constitution. Police used this tactic to prevent protests from taking place. They often released the detainees after a few hours but reportedly sometimes kept them for days. For example, on March 30, police detained up to 14 members of the antigovernment group "Revolutionary Movement of Angola." Police reportedly picked up prominent members of the movement early in the morning as they were en route to a protest planned for later that morning. Police reportedly shuttled the protesters from one station to another, took them on long drives, and used other tactics to hold them throughout the day. Police released all of the detained protesters that same night or early the next morning (see section 2.b.).

Role of the Police and Security Apparatus

The national police, controlled by the ministry of interior, are responsible for internal security and law enforcement. The state intelligence and security service reports to the presidency and investigates sensitive state security matters. The Angolan Armed Forces (FAA) are responsible for external security but also had domestic security responsibilities, including border security, expulsion of irregular immigrants, and small-scale actions against the Front for the Liberation of the Enclave of Cabinda (FLEC) separatists in Cabinda.

Civilian authorities maintained effective control over the FAA and the national police, and the government had mechanisms to investigate and punish abuse and corruption. The security forces generally were effective, although sometimes brutal, at maintaining stability. The national police and FAA have internal mechanisms to investigate security force abuses, and the government provided some training to reform the security forces.

Other than personnel assigned to elite units, police were poorly paid, and the practice of supplementing income through extortion of civilians was widespread. Corruption and impunity remained serious problems. A domestic NGO reported that police throughout the country were abusive and created a gulf between authority figures and the people they are meant to protect. The national police handled most complaints internally through opaque disciplinary procedures, which sometimes led to formal punishment, including dismissal. The government had not established regular or transparent mechanisms to expedite investigations and punish alleged offenders, and it rarely disclosed publicly the results of internal investigations.

Police participated in professional training with foreign law enforcement officials from several countries in the region.

Arrest Procedures and Treatment While in Detention

Prior to an arrest, the law requires a judge or magistrate to issue a warrant, although a person caught committing a crime may be arrested immediately without a warrant. Security force personnel, however, did not always procure arrest warrants before detaining persons.

Police can legally detain an individual under reasonable suspicion for six hours without evidence of a crime.

The law states detainees cannot be held longer than 24 hours without leveling charges, but this law was not respected.

The constitution provides the right to prompt judicial determination of the detention's legality, but authorities often did not respect this right.

The law mandates that detainees be informed of charges against them within five days. In certain cases the prosecutor may permit the suspect to return home and provide a warrant of surveillance to local police, and this provision was generally observed.

For misdemeanors the suspect may be detained for 30 days before trial. For felonies, the prosecutor may prolong pretrial detention up to 45 days. Pretrial detention may be prolonged by court order while officials build their case. Requests to prolong pretrial detention are not made public, which made it difficult to determine whether authorities exceeded the limits. Civil society organizations faced difficulties in contacting detainees, and prison authorities undermined civil society work in the prisons.

A functioning but ineffective bail system, widely used for minor crimes, existed. Prisoners and their families reported that prison officials demanded bribes to release prisoners. Prisoners were allowed access to a lawyer, although this did not always happen.

The law mandates access to legal counsel for detainees and states that indigent detainees should be provided a lawyer by the state. These rights often were not respected, in part due to the shortage of legal professionals. Reportedly, 95 percent of lawyers nationwide were based in Luanda, implying an even greater shortage in rural areas. The law allows family members prompt access to detainees, but courts occasionally ignored this right or made it conditional upon payment of a bribe.

Arbitrary Arrest: Unlawful arrest and detention remained serious problems. NGOs continued efforts to secure the release of persons detained illegally. Security officials arbitrarily arrested groups or individuals not aligned with the ruling MPLA.

In June the attorney general's office opened criminal proceedings against the online news blog Club-K because of articles the blog had run accusing the attorney general of money laundering and fraud. The blog was operated outside of the country, and its directors and owners were not publicly known. The attorney general named a Club-K journalist and an editor as defendants in the case even though neither had any connection to the articles in question. Authorities forced the men to give depositions on numerous occasions and denied them the right to leave the country for a period of more than a month.

Several civil society and political party representatives reported incidents of security forces detaining Cabinda residents suspected of FLEC activity or collaboration. One political party representative claimed that security forces were holding at least 29 alleged FLEC members without charging them; some civil society figures put the number closer to 50. Attempts to meet with government representatives in Cabinda were unsuccessful, but several government officials publicly described conditions in Cabinda as being largely positive and peaceful during media interviews throughout the year.

Pretrial Detention: Excessively long pretrial detention continued to be a serious problem. An inadequate number of judges and poor communication among authorities contributed to the problem. Police beat and then released detainees rather than prepare a formal court case. In some cases authorities held inmates in prison for up to two years before their trials began. The ministry of interior reported that over 40 percent of inmates were pretrial detainees, many of whom had not been formally charged. The government often did not release detainees who had been held beyond the legal time limit, claiming that previous releases of pretrial detainees had resulted in an increase in crime.

e. Denial of Fair Public Trial

Although the constitution provides for an independent judiciary, the judiciary remained understaffed, inefficient, corrupt (see section 4), and subject to executive and political influence. While the law provides for an independent and impartial judiciary in civil matters, the judiciary reportedly encountered political interference.

There were long trial delays at the Supreme Court. Criminal courts also had a large backlog of cases, which resulted in major delays in hearings. There were only 19 municipal courts for 163 municipalities. In several instances the government would choose to expedite a case when it stood to gain by winning.

Informal courts remained the principal institutions through which citizens resolved conflicts in rural areas. Each community in which they were located established local rules. Traditional leaders also heard and decided local cases. These informal systems did not provide citizens with the same rights to a fair trial as the formal legal system.

Most municipalities did not have prosecutors or judges. Local police often served as investigator, prosecutor, and judge. Both the national police and the FAA have internal court systems that generally remained closed to outside scrutiny. Although members of these organizations can be tried under their internal regulations, cases that include violations of criminal or civil laws can also fall under the jurisdiction of provincial courts.

Trial Procedures

Although the law provides for the right to a fair trial, the government did not always respect this right. Suspects must be in the presence of a judge and defense attorney when charged. Defendants have the right to be informed within five days of the charges levied against them, although this right is not always respected. It was not known if they had the right to interpretation. Defendants are presumed innocent until convicted. By law trials are usually public, although each court has the right to close proceedings. Juries are not used. Defendants have the right to be present and consult with an attorney in a timely manner. The law requires that an attorney be provided at public expense if an indigent defendant faces serious criminal charges. Outside of Luanda the public defender was generally not a trained attorney due to shortages in qualified personnel. Defendants do not have the right to confront their accusers. They may question witnesses against them and present witnesses and evidence on their own behalf. In general defendants had enough time and facilities to prepare a defense. The government did not always respect all of these rights. It was not known whether defendants were generally compelled to testify or confess guilt; however, in at least one case on July 23, the national directorate for investigative and penal action compelled a defendant to act as a state witness against himself in a criminal complaint.

Defendants and their attorneys have the right to access government-held evidence relevant to their cases. In addition defendants have the right to appeal. Authorities did not always respect these rights.

The law extends to all citizens. A separate court under the ministry of justice and human rights is designated for children's affairs. It functions as part of Luanda's provincial court system. The juvenile court also hears cases of minors between the ages of 12 and 16 accused of committing a criminal offense. Minors over the age of 16 accused of committing a criminal offense are tried in regular courts. In many rural provinces, there is no provision for juvenile courts, so offenders as young as 12 can be tried as adults. In many cases traditional leaders (known as "sobas") have state authority to resolve disputes and determine punishments for criminal offences, including offences committed by juveniles. The law is unclear where the authority of the soba ends and that of the official legal system begins.

The president appoints Supreme Court justices for life terms without confirmation by the national assembly. The Supreme Court generally heard cases concerning alleged political and security crimes.

Political Prisoners and Detainees

There were reports of political prisoners. At the beginning of the year, at least three (and perhaps as many as eight) political activists from the Movement for Autonomy and Independence of the Lundas remained imprisoned for crimes against state security and instigating a rebellion, even though the state security law under which they were convicted had been repealed. Secretary of State for Human Rights Bento Bembe acknowledged the unlawful detention of these activists in early November and had successfully gained their release by the middle of the month. It was unclear whether the government permitted access to these prisoners while they were in prison, or whether any attempts were made by international humanitarian organizations to visit them.

Civil Judicial Procedures and Remedies

Damages for human rights violations could be sought in municipal or provincial courts and appealed to the Supreme Court. No known cases were decided in the plaintiffs favor during the year.

Property Restitution

The law requires that citizens cannot be relocated without being provided fair compensation. As in previous years, however, authorities relocated several thousand persons during the year; most did not receive fair compensation (see section 1.f.). Under the constitution all untitled land belongs to the state. The state claimed many of the former residents did not have clear title to their dwellings, which made them illegally constructed.

The government exercised eminent domain to destroy private homes. Titled homeowners were not compensated at fair market value for the loss of their residences or land. Untitled homeowners often received no compensation.

f. Arbitrary Interference with Privacy, Family, Home, or Correspondence

The constitution and law prohibit such actions, but the government did not always respect these prohibitions. For example, civil organizations and politically active individuals, including government critics, members of opposition parties, and journalists, complained that the government maintained surveillance of their activities and membership. These groups also frequently complained of threats and harassment based on their affiliations to groups that are nominally or explicitly antigovernment.

Usually accompanied by police and military personnel, authorities destroyed several thousand homes throughout the country, often with little advance notice. For example, on February 1, a heavily armed police contingent, including several police helicopters, accompanied several teams of bulldozers as they began leveling the Maiombe neighborhood in the Luanda suburb of Cacuaco. In total authorities demolished more than 5,000 homes and forcibly relocated 1,700 families. The families were reportedly to be given 100 to 150 square foot plots of land in a nearby field; as of year's end all or nearly all families had received a plot, although the area had little or no access to water, electricity, health services, schools, or other essential public goods.

According to HRW and SOS Habitat, a local NGO, authorities gave the Maiombe residents little or no advanced notice of the government's plans to level the area, nor did they provide families adequate time to remove their personal possessions before the heavy machinery began its work. Police arrested those who tried to protest the destruction on charges of disobedience and illegal land operation. Nearly 100 persons were convicted and given sentences of up to eight months in prison, although HRW claimed the trials did not meet international due process standards and that the defendants were unable to challenge the charges made against them or to call witnesses in their defense. A representative from HRW was detained "for her own protection" when she tried to visit the site. On a separate occasion, police prevented the president of the largest opposition party from visiting Maiombe, again claiming that it was to protect him from potentially being attacked by residents of the area.

Section 2. Respect for Civil Liberties, Including:

a. Freedom of Speech and Press

The constitution and law provide for freedom of speech and press; however, state dominance of most media outlets and self-censorship by journalists limited these rights. There was minimal private media outside of Luanda.

<u>Freedom of Speech</u>: Individuals reported practicing self-censorship but generally were able to criticize the government without fear of direct reprisal. The government engaged in economic coercion and subtle repression, often in the form of offering bribes or withdrawing business or job opportunities, to discourage criticism. Multiple sources reported that citizens often curtailed their support of an opposition political party because they would suffer reprisals from MPLA supporters.

On September 19, authorities prevented a youth group from holding an antigovernment protest in Luanda. Police arrived at the protest routes early and arrested, detained, or intimidated more than 20 protesters. Police issued a verbal warning that the protest did not meet the technical requirements to proceed, but reportedly refused to put the information in writing when requested to do so. According to the protesters, this occurred because the protesters did not actually break any laws when organizing their event.

<u>Press Freedoms</u>: There were 13 privately owned weekly newspapers and eight Luanda-based commercial radio stations. All but one of these publications, *Folha 8*, were rumored to be owned by groups or individuals tied to the government. Nongovernment radio stations could broadcast only in provinces where they physically established antennas. The government allowed only government-owned Radio Nacional to use repeaters to expand signal reach and was thus the only station broadcasting in much of the country. Most private radio stations could reach audiences only in Luanda. Radio Mais, whose ownership included individuals associated with the ruling party, also broadcast in Huambo and Benguela. Radio 2000, whose owners also were believed to be connected to the ruling party, operated in Huila. Privately owned Radio Comercial operated in Cabinda but suspended operations in November 2012 for financial reasons.

Private radio and print media criticized the government openly and harshly, but sometimes faced repercussions for doing so. Authorities occasionally threatened journalists and publishers with harassment and/or arrest for printing critical stories, especially those which centered on the president or his family. On May 15, the Ministry for Social Communication issued letters to radio station Radio Despertar (linked to political opposition party UNITA) and newspaper *Folha 8* (linked to political opposition party CASA-CE), warning them to cease putting out "insults and defamatory remarks" about government institutions and the leaders who run them. The ministry threatened to shut down the radio station and newspaper if they did not cooperate with the terms of the letter. Both operations were open at year's end, as the ministry did not follow through with the threats.

Official news outlets, including Angolan Public Television, Radio Nacional, and the *Jornal de Angola*, favored the ruling party and gave only limited coverage to opposition political parties and civil society organizations.

Violence and Harassment: During the year authorities arrested, harassed, and intimidated journalists. For example, in mid-July the attorney general's office brought libel and slander cases against a reporter and editor of a popular online news blog because of the blog's regular reporting on cases of alleged police torture and allegations of corruption against the attorney general. The two individuals were required to give testimony and temporarily prevented from leaving the country, even though neither had direct links to the articles in question.

On September 20, police detained and physically abused three journalists, including the well-known human rights defender Rafael Marques, for over four hours without pressing charges. The journalists were interviewing a group of young antigovernment protesters who had just been released from overnight detention when police officers quickly surrounded the group of journalists and protesters and apprehended them. The officers reportedly beat the journalists and damaged their equipment, then released them several hours later after claiming their detention had been a mistake. The journalists believed the police knew exactly who they were apprehending and that the detention was an attempt to intimidate the journalists and the protestors.

Censorship or Content Restrictions: Journalists practiced self-censorship.

There were reports that security forces interfered with journalists' and civic activists' attempts to take pictures or video during the year. For example, on August 31, police in Cafunfo, Lunda Norte, allegedly collected the computers, mobile phones, and digital cameras of more than 345 citizens (including journalists and civil society representatives) to check whether any had images of women who had recently been found ritualistically killed and mutilated. According to an NGO source, police actions were not due to an ongoing murder investigation but because they were trying to prevent the images from provoking human rights concerns.

During the year security guards and signs warned visitors not to take photographs of any government-affiliated buildings or persons because security forces might seize their cameras or detain them. Police also regularly confiscated or damaged mobile phones and cameras of people who were documenting police abuse or mistreatment.

The minister of social communication, the spokesperson of the presidency, and the national director of information maintained significant decision-making authority over the media. It was commonly understood that these individuals actively vetted news stories in the state-controlled print, television, and radio media, and even exercised considerable authority over non-state media controlled by figures close to the government. Stories critical of President dos Santos or the MPLA were not published or broadcast by these organs.

The government also restricted nationwide independent broadcasting through licensing laws. In December 2012 Radio Ecclesia dropped its petition to expand broadcast coverage to provinces outside of Luanda. More than one source reported that Radio Ecclesia, which is operated by the Roman Catholic Church and was once considered to be a good source of nonpartisan information, decreased its coverage of controversial news topics in favor of softer programming that generally favored the government.

Libel Laws/National Security: Defamation is a crime punishable by imprisonment or a fine, and defendants have the burden of proving their innocence by providing evidence of the validity of the allegedly damaging material.

On September 12, police arrested Manuel Nito Alves in the Luanda suburb of Viana for printing t-shirts with slogans opposing the president and for inciting violence. The t-shirts stated that "32 is Enough," a popular slogan among antigovernment youth that references the many years that President dos Santos has been in power. The shirt also called dos Santos a "Gross Dictator," and quoted the headline of a controversial newspaper article, "When War is Urgent and Necessary in Angola." The shirts apparently were printed for individuals to wear during an antigovernment demonstration scheduled one week later. Police detained Alves for nearly two months before releasing him on bail.

Internet Freedom

There were no government restrictions on access to the internet or credible reports the government monitored e-mail or internet chat rooms without judicial oversight. According to the International Telecommunication Union, in 2012 approximately 17 percent of individuals used the internet.

Academic Freedom and Cultural Events

There were no government restrictions on academic freedom or cultural events.

b. Freedom of Peaceful Assembly and Association

Freedom of Assembly

Although the constitution and law provide for the right of assembly, the government regularly restricted this right. At least 10 public demonstrations took place during the year; police detained persons during each of these demonstrations.

The law requires written notification to the local administrator and police three days before public assemblies are to be held, but it does not require government permission for such events. The government at times prohibited events based on perceived or claimed security considerations. Participants potentially were liable for "offenses against the honor and consideration due to persons and to organs of sovereignty." Police and administrators did not interfere with progovernment gatherings. Nonpartisan groups intending to criticize the government or government leaders, however, often met a heavy police presence and government excuses preventing them from carrying out the event. Usually authorities claimed that the timing or venue requested was problematic or that the proper authorities had not received notification.

During the year activists suffered intimidation, including anonymous death threats, because of their involvement in public demonstrations. For example, on March 30, police detained several would-be protesters before they reached a designated rally point. Police reportedly went to protesters' homes and neighborhoods and waited for the protesters to begin heading towards the rally point, then preemptively detained them throughout the day. Members of the antigovernment youth protest group complained that on numerous occasions police threatened to "take them to a warehouse," "hurt them badly," or carry out other extrajudicial punishments if they did not discontinue their association with the protest movement. Similarly, on November 23, according to press reports, police detained 292 persons ahead of and during protests across the country.

Freedom of Association

The constitution and law provide for the right of association, and the government generally respected this right. Nevertheless, extensive and unexplained delays in the NGO registration process continued to be a problem. According to a 2011 survey, the ministry of justice and human rights properly certified approximately

70 percent of the NGOs operating in the country. The rest were unable to obtain certification but were allowed to operate.

The government sometimes arbitrarily restricted the activities of NGOs. One NGO reported that the government welcomed activities focused on health or education but threatened to close the NGO when it engaged in activities on political awareness and civil rights.

The government at times arbitrarily restricted the activities of associations it considered subversive by refusing to grant permits for organized activities. During the year opposition parties generally were permitted to organize and hold meetings; however, opposition officials continued to report obstructions to the free exercise of their parties' right to meet. For example, local authorities threatened members who attended such meetings.

c. Freedom of Religion

See the Department of State's *International Religious Freedom Report* at www.state.gov/j/drl/irf/rpt/.

d. Freedom of Movement, Internally Displaced Persons, Protection of Refugees, and Stateless Persons

The constitution and law provide for freedom of internal movement, foreign travel, emigration, and repatriation; however, the government at times restricted these rights. The government cooperated with the Office of the UN High Commissioner for Refugees (UNHCR), the International Organization for Migration, and other humanitarian organizations in providing protection and assistance to internally displaced persons, refugees, asylum seekers, and other persons of concern. Several sources, however, claimed that security forces frequently abused irregular migrants in the border region shared with the DRC.

In-country Movement: Extortion and harassment at government checkpoints in rural areas and at provincial and international border checkpoints interfered with the right to travel. During the year, however, the government decreased checkpoints between provinces. Extortion by police was routine in cities on major commercial routes. The government and private security companies restricted access to the areas around designated diamond concessions. The government regularly denied citizens living near concession areas access for any purpose, even for obtaining water.

Land mines and other ERW remaining from the civil war continued to impede freedom of movement in rural areas.

Internally Displaced Persons (IDPs)

Officially there were no longer significant numbers of IDPs. The majority of persons previously considered IDPs either returned home or did not intend to return to their area of origin, as many considered their new locations to be home. Some stated a lack of physical infrastructure, government services such as medical care, and the presence of land mines were major deterrents to their return.

In the capital, where there is lack of clarity over land possession and ownership, the government forcibly evicted many poor and vulnerable individuals, including former displaced persons who decided to remain. Most IDPs who never returned to the countryside stayed in the peripheries of Luanda or provincial towns. With few job skills and limited education, most could not find jobs in the formal market. Many worked in the informal economy and lived in slums without access to adequate social services, such as housing, education, water, and sanitation and health services. Although they did not face specific discrimination and their living conditions were broadly the same as those of the nondisplaced population, many former IDPs were among the poorest and remained excluded from mechanisms to protect their rights.

The ministry of assistance and social reinsertion has primary responsibility for returnees and any remaining IDPs as well as housing and resettlement programs, but its efforts remained inadequate. The ministry delegated primary responsibility to provincial governments for the safe, voluntary resettlement of IDPs in areas cleared of mines and with access to water, arable land, markets, and adequate state administration. Their efforts also were largely inadequate to meet these needs.

The government did not restrict aid efforts by international humanitarian groups and allowed international organizations access to refugee camps, returnee welcome centers, and border crossings to conduct assessment missions.

Protection of Refugees

Government officials and returning Angolan refugees reported that returnees received some assistance from the ministry of assistance and social reinsertion and international organizations, but they continued to require legal assistance to regularize their status and to obtain supplies to restart their careers, education and language training, agricultural supplies, and housing materials. During the year the ministry assisted at least 800 families returning from Namibia with shelter, professional kits, clothing, and in some cases land for agricultural purposes so families could sustain themselves in the long run.

In 2009 the government and the UNHCR resumed joint efforts to repatriate thousands of refugees remaining outside the country since the civil war. These efforts continued even after June 2012 when the UNHCR and regional governments agreed to a cessation of prima facie refugee status for Angolans on the grounds that asylum and protection for most Angolans was no longer required. During the year Angolan refugees returned voluntarily from Namibia, Zambia, the Republic of the Congo, and the DRC. According to the UNHCR, more than 117,000 Angolan refugees or persons in a refugee-like situation remained in neighboring countries as of January. The government cooperated with the UNHCR on voluntary refugee repatriation and reintegration programs, but operations were significantly delayed due to funding constraints and lack of reintegration support to returnees.

Access to Asylum: The law provides vague rules for the granting of asylum or refugee status, and the government has established a system for providing protection to refugees. During the year the government created an inter-ministerial commission to look into rewriting the refugee and asylum laws and stopped granting refugee status or asylum during this period. On June 7, the minister of interior stated that Angola was host to 29,092 refugees and asylum seekers, of which 15,842 were legalized and 13,250 had cases pending. The minister also claimed that most foreign nationals seeking asylum in the country do it with an interest in engaging in trade, illegal diamond exploration, the sale of diamonds, and "other types of crimes and indecent behavior."

Refoulement: The government provided some protection against the expulsion or return of refugees to countries where their lives or freedom would be threatened on account of their race, religion, nationality, membership in a particular social group, or political opinion.

Employment: There were no formal restrictions on a refugee's ability to seek employment. Refugees sometimes faced difficulty obtaining employment due to a lack of legal documents required to work in the formal sector and difficulty in obtaining such documents. These difficulties were compounded by a general lack of acceptance of the refugee card and a lack of knowledge about the rights it was intended to safeguard.

Access to Basic Services: Persons with recognized refugee status could take advantage of public services, but refugees at times faced difficulty obtaining access to public services such as health care and education due to a lack of legal documents. Corruption by officials compounded these difficulties.

Section 3. Respect for Political Rights: The Right of Citizens to Change Their Government

The constitution and law provide citizens with the right to change their government peacefully. In August 2012 citizens exercised the right to elect legislative representatives and the president. The constitution calls for the first-ever elections at the municipal and provincial levels to happen according to the principle of "gradualism," where local elections are to be held in provinces and municipalities based on a variable timeline. The right to elect local leaders remained restricted, and elections did not occur at the provincial or municipal levels.

Elections and Political Participation

Recent Elections: In August 2012 the government held legislative elections and the country's first postwar presidential election. According to the constitution passed in 2010, presidential and legislative elections should be held every five years. The ruling MPLA won 71.8 percent of the vote in the legislative elections. Domestic and international observers reported polling throughout the country was peaceful and generally credible, although the ruling party enjoyed advantages due to state control of major media and other resources. Opposition parties criticized many aspects of the electoral process, including ruling party control of the major media, late disbursement of public campaign funds, the national electoral commission's failure to accredit some opposition and civil society electoral observers, and the large number of individuals unable to vote because they were either were unregistered or were registered in a location far from their residences. These and other irregularities led to an abstention rate of 37 percent, much higher than the 13 percent abstention rate recorded in the 2008 legislative elections. Opposition parties contested the electoral results but accepted their seats in the national assembly. In September 2012 the constitutional court rejected opposition appeals and certified the election results as free and fair.

Political Parties: The ruling MPLA party dominated all political institutions. Political power was concentrated in the presidency and the council of ministers, through which the president exercised executive power. The council can enact laws, decrees, and resolutions, assuming most functions normally associated with the legislative branch. The national assembly consists of 220 deputies elected under a party list proportional representation system. This body has the authority to draft, debate, and pass legislation, but the executive branch often proposed and drafted legislation for the assembly's approval. After the August 2012 legislative elections, opposition deputies held 20 percent of parliamentary seats, a 7 percent increase from 2008.

Opposition parties stated their members were subject to harassment, intimidation, and assault by MPLA supporters. UNITA continued to argue that the MPLA had not lived up to the terms of the 2002 peace accord, and former combatants lacked the social services and assistance needed to reintegrate into society. Former combatants also reported difficulties obtaining pensions due to bureaucratic delays or discrimination. During the year UNITA reported that its members suffered intimidation and harassment. For example, in September members of UNITA claimed the MPLA set up a road block to prevent UNITA members from returning from a political rally. UNITA further claimed that FAA members, police, and the local government administrator (who is from the MPLA) assisted in manning the road block. A fight ensued when the UNITA supporters tried to move past the illegal road block, reportedly leaving some UNITA equipment damaged and at least one supporter hospitalized.

Participation of Women and Minorities: Of the 220 deputies in the national assembly, 74 were women. Two women served as governors (out of 18 nationwide), and eight women were cabinet ministers (out of 35).

The country has three dominant linguistic groups: the Ovimbundu, Mbundu, and Bakongo, which together constitute approximately 77 percent of the population. All were represented in government, as were other groups. Political parties must be represented in all 18 provinces, but only the MPLA and UNITA (and CASA-CE to a lesser extent) had truly national constituencies. By law no political party could limit party membership based on ethnicity, race, or gender.

Section 4. Corruption and Lack of Transparency in Government

Although the law provides criminal penalties for official corruption, the government did not implement these laws effectively, and local and international

NGOs and media sources reported that officials engaged in corrupt practices with impunity.

Corruption: Government corruption at all levels was endemic. The country does not have a special entity mandated with the responsibility of combating corruption. Public prosecutions were rare. During the year the government did not charge or prosecute any high-level official for corruption. The national criminal investigation department of the national police also investigated some cases.

Government corruption was widespread, and accountability was limited due to a lack of checks and balances, lack of institutional capacity, and a culture of impunity. The judiciary was corrupt and subject to political influence and conflict of interest.

The attorney general's office, national assembly, financial court, supreme court, and national directorate of inspection and investigation of economic activities (DNIIAE) were all responsible for combating corruption. The attorney general's office had the authority to initiate investigations into potential cases of corruption at high levels. The DNIIAE did so at lower levels. The court system had responsibility for convicting and punishing corruption cases.

As in previous years, there were credible reports that government officials used their political positions to profit from business deals. For example, the daughter of Jose Maria, the head of the FAA's military intelligence and security directorate, reportedly owned a company that had millions of dollars in contracts with the FAA. The commander-general of the national police reportedly owned a company that sells weapons to the national police.

The business climate continued to favor those connected to the government, including members of the president's family. In March *Forbes* magazine listed Isabel dos Santos, daughter of President dos Santos, as Africa's youngest billionaire with a net worth of more than two billion dollars. In August *Forbes* increased its estimate of her wealth to more than three billion dollars, and claimed that every one of her major investments "stems either from taking a chunk of a company that wants to do business in the country or from a stroke of the president's pen that cut her into the action."

Government ministers and other high-level officials commonly and openly owned interests in companies regulated by or doing business with their respective ministries. There are laws and regulations regarding conflict of interest, but they were not enforced. Petty corruption among police, teachers, and other government employees was widespread. Police extorted money from citizens and refugees, and prison officials extorted money from family members of inmates (see sections 1.c., 1.d., and 2.d.).

In February the Swiss NGO Berne Declaration reported on potentially illicit business dealings between Trafigura, the third largest Swiss company, and Leopoldino Fragoso do Nascimento "Dino," a general in the FAA and an advisor to President dos Santos. According to the NGO, Claude Dauphin, a founding stakeholder in Trafigura, and Dino do Nascimento are joint shareholders in and directors of a company that had monopolistic contracts worth $3.3 billion with the Angolan state-owned oil company Sonangol. The NGO also detailed several other business ventures in Angola between Trafigura and various holding companies that are wholly or partially owned by Dino do Nascimento and other high ranking government officials, including Vice President Manuel Vicente and the head of state security, General Manuel "Kopelipa" Helder Vieira Dias Junior.

On July 26, a judge sentenced Joaquim Ribeiro, the former commander of the Luanda Provincial Police--who was under investigation for embezzling public funds and ordering the killing of a police officer--to 15 years in prison and a fine of nearly 3.2 million kwanzas ($33,684) in fines for his role in the crimes. Several other culprits were given sentences ranging from two to 14 years' imprisonment.

In April the Angolan human rights organization Maos Livres (Open Hands) and the London-based Corruption Watch UK, reported on a corrupt debt repayment deal between Angola and Russia that ran from 1996-2004. Although the case itself, known widely as "Angolagate," was not new, the authors claimed to have identified new information about the way the deal was carried out and who the primary players were. The report alleges that several high-level officials, including President dos Santos, were among a small group of beneficiaries who illegally earned at least $386 million from the deal. It identified an additional $400 million in unaccounted funds that likely went to pay off other unknown insider beneficiaries. The report also implicates the Swiss Banking Corporation (which later merged with the Swiss banking giant UBS) as being complicit in the deal, and called on the governments of Angola, Switzerland, and several EU states to investigate the "Angolagate" scandal based on the information uncovered. By year's end, no known action had been taken.

Whistleblower Protection: The country has no explicit whistleblower laws, although Article 73 of the constitution does state that citizens have a right to petition, denounce, and present legal complaints in defense of their rights, of the constitution and other laws, and in defense of general interests.

Financial Disclosure: In 2010 the national assembly approved a law on public probity, which requires most government officials to declare their assets to the attorney general. However, no officials made information available to the public during the year, and the president, vice president, and president of the national assembly are exempt from these requirements. The law stipulates that nonexempt government officials declare all real estate holdings, household goods, livestock, cash assets, land titles, and stock holdings. Declarations are to include all assets in country and overseas. The law does not cover spouses and children. Nonexempt government officials are to make a new declaration within 30 days of assuming a new post and every two years thereafter. The law does not stipulate that a new declaration be made upon leaving office but does state that officials must return all government property within 60 days. Penalties for noncompliance vary depending on which section of the law was violated but include removal from office, a bar from government work for three to five years, a bar from contracting with the government for three years, repayment of the illicitly gained assets, and a fine of up to 100 times the value of the accepted bribe. The national office of economic police is responsible for investigating violations of this law, as well as other financial and economic crimes, and then referring them to the Financial Court for prosecution. There were no known cases related to this law during the year.

The government publicly discloses its national budget on an annual basis, including incomes and expenditures, but fiscal data is not complete, accurate, or reliable. Revenue flows from the oil sector to the budget are hard to track, as transfers from Sonangol, the state-owned oil company, to the state treasury are delayed and sporadic. The government reportedly was taking measures to address these shortcomings and successfully completed its second technical review after completing its stand-by arrangement with the IMF in March 2012. Sonangol phased out most, but not all, of its quasi-fiscal activities.

The government published online a detailed block-by-block accounting of the monthly revenues it received from Sonangol's oil production. It continued to withhold, however, financial information about the sale price of offshore oil blocks sold in 2011. The bonuses that oil companies pay for block purchases, which are paid on top of the bid price, reportedly reach into the tens of millions of dollars, and the blocks themselves have sold for billions of dollars. There also continued to be a significant lack of transparency in the government's overall procurement and use of loans received from private banks and foreign governments.

To monitor and control expenditures more effectively, the ministry of finance continued implementation of the integrated financial system, designed to record all central government expenditures.

The financial statements of Endiama, the state diamond parastatal, were not made public. Serious transparency problems remained in the diamond industry, particularly regarding allocation of exploration, production, and purchasing rights and reporting of revenues. In April a leading human rights activist accused the chief executive officer of Endiama of corruption and "self-dealing" in the diamond trade by owning 99 percent of a company that trades with Endiama.

In June the government announced that President dos Santos' son, Jose Filomeno "Zenu" dos Santos, would take over as the chair of the country's five billion dollar sovereign wealth fund. The fund is tasked with investing some of the country's oil wealth in infrastructure and social development projects, although at year's end no funds had yet been invested. In December 2012 an opposition political party filed a complaint with the Constitutional Court challenging the constitutionality of the presidential decree that created the fund. The complaint was not that the country should not have such a fund, but rather that dos Santos as president could not create it without authorization from the national assembly. The Constitutional Court declared on February 8 that the act was constitutional. In its press release, the court explained that "since the fund is a public administration structure, it depends exclusively on the president of the republic," and therefore he is permitted to create it and run it as he sees fit.

Public Access to Information: The law provides for public access to government information. While the amount of information posted on government websites gradually increased, it remained limited. Laws are made public by being published in the official gazette. The publication can be purchased for a small fee but was not available online in its entirety. In general the government was not responsive to requests for information, and it was sometimes unclear what information the government considered public versus private.

Section 5. Governmental Attitude Regarding International and Nongovernmental Investigation of Alleged Violations of Human Rights

A variety of domestic and international human rights groups operated throughout the country. Some of those investigating government corruption and human rights abuses alleged government interference in their activities. Civil society organizations faced difficulties in contacting detainees, and prison authorities undermined civil society work in the prisons.

Local NGOs promoted and defended human rights to the extent possible during the year by asserting constitutional rights, protesting labor conditions, providing free legal counsel, lobbying government officials, and publishing investigative reports.

The Law of Association requires NGOs to specify their mandate and areas of activity. The government used this provision to prevent or discourage established NGOs from engaging in certain activities, especially those that were politically sensitive. Government officials threatened to ban those NGOs it determined to be operating outside their mandate or not effectively working on the specific issues they were created to address. NGO leaders suspected the motive was to silence their criticism. No NGOs were banned during the year.

The government allowed local NGOs to carry out human rights-related work, but many NGOs were forced to limit the scope of their work because they faced problems registering, were subject to subtle forms of intimidation, and risked more serious forms of harassment and closure.

The government arrested and harassed NGO workers. For example, on September 2, authorities forced a member of Omunga, a human rights NGO based in Benguela Province, to stop his car. They then allegedly put a gun to the activist's head and told him that if he valued his life, he would stop supporting a group of striking grocery store workers.

The government criticized domestic and international NGOs.

There were reports of police or military presence at community meetings with international NGOs, especially in Cabinda.

Mpalabanda, a civil society organization formerly based in Cabinda, remained banned. By year's end the Supreme Court had not responded to a petition to reexamine the ban.

UN and Other International Bodies: The government cooperated with international governmental organizations and permitted visits by UN representatives. In 2008 the UN Human Rights Office closed following a government decision not to grant a full mandate to the office. UNHCHR Navi Pillay visited the country in April and met with President dos Santos, several ministers, senior officials, the governor of

Lunda Norte, and the Attorney General's Office. Authorities allowed Pillay and other UN officials to meet with civil society groups and travel to a border crossing between Angola and the DRC. In her report, Pillay complimented the government on the progress since the end of the civil war, particularly in infrastructure improvements. She also highlighted persistent concerns including the growing disparity between rich and poor, and the harsh methods the government had used to evict people from land earmarked for development. She encouraged the government to strengthen the human rights protections of its citizens and establish a National Human Rights Institution in accordance with the Paris Principles, and offered to support the appointment of a UN Human Rights Advisor to the country.

Some international NGOs reported long delays in obtaining visas, although the delays were not significantly longer than those experienced by other foreigners.

Government Human Rights Bodies: In July the Inter-Ministerial Commission for the Writing of Human Rights Reports (CIERDH) held a series of conferences and workshops aimed at increasing awareness of human rights in the country. The commission invited members of civil society and the international community to attend the conferences, and also invited civil society to nominate representatives to serve on the commission itself. CIERDH is comprised entirely of representatives from various government ministries and funded by the state. It has strong leadership and several quality members, and has proven to be a reasonably effective organization that is strengthening over time. Leading civil society members decided not to participate on the commission because they did not believe it was independent or effective.

Section 6. Discrimination, Societal Abuses, and Trafficking in Persons

The constitution and law prohibit discrimination based on race, gender, religion, disability, language, or social status, but not sexual orientation or gender identity; however, the government did not effectively enforce these prohibitions. Violence and discrimination against women, child abuse, child prostitution, trafficking in persons, and discrimination against persons with disabilities were problems.

Women

Rape and Domestic Violence: Rape, including spousal rape, is illegal and punishable by up to eight years' imprisonment; however, limited investigative resources, poor forensic capabilities, and an ineffective judicial system prevented prosecution of most cases. The ministry of justice and human rights worked with the ministry of interior to increase the number of female police officers and to improve police response to rape allegations.

The National Assembly passed a law against domestic violence in 2011, although implementation remained a problem. Domestic violence against women, including spousal abuse, was pervasive in both urban and rural areas. In December 2012 the government announced a nationwide campaign entitled "Zero Tolerance for Gender and Sexual Based Violence." The campaign included full-page anti-domestic violence advertisements in the national newspaper, government-sponsored rallies and marches against domestic violence, and other measures aimed at raising awareness about and changing a culture of domestic violence.

The government reported it had 27 domestic violence counseling centers, seven other shelters, and various treatment centers throughout the country. The Organization of Angolan Women, a political association affiliated with the ruling MPLA, announced in August that it had recorded more than 13,000 cases of domestic abuse nationwide from May through July. It called for more studies into the causes of domestic violence as well as more shelters to help victims. The ministry maintained a program with the Angolan Bar Association to give free legal assistance to abused women and established counseling centers to help families cope with domestic abuse. Statistics on prosecutions for violence against women were not available.

Harmful Traditional Practices: A handful of reports from provinces bordering the DRC stated that societal violence against elderly persons and rural and impoverished women and children occurred, with most cases stemming from accusations of witchcraft. The leader of a human rights NGO in Lunda Norte reported at least six women were ritualistically killed during the year. He stated that certain diamond merchants believed that ritualistically killing these women, and sometimes harvesting parts of their bodies, would help bring them good luck in the diamond fields. He also believed that employees of mine security companies were involved in the killings. Police arrested at least one suspect in the case, although no information about his trial was available.

Female Genital Mutilation (FGM/Cutting): FGM/C was not considered a widespread practice, although there were reports of instances in eastern provinces. The government acknowledged FGM/C as a human rights concern and pledged to address the practice but did not provide specifics.

Sexual Harassment: Sexual harassment was common and not illegal. Such cases may be prosecuted under assault and battery and defamation statutes.

Reproductive Rights: Couples and individuals may decide freely and responsibly the number, spacing, and timing of their children, and they had access to the information and means to do so free from discrimination, coercion, and violence. Women had access to contraception. According to a UN study, just 7 percent of rural women and 17 percent of urban women used a modern method of contraception. A 2009 study found 47 percent of women and girls who gave birth had four or more prenatal consultations. Of them, approximately 67 percent of women and girls saw a qualified health provider at least once, 49 percent of births were attended by skilled health personnel, and 42 percent gave birth in a medical center. According to UN estimates, the maternal mortality ratio in 2010 was 450 deaths per 100,000 live births. High maternal mortality was likely due to inadequate access to health facilities before, during, and after giving birth, and early pregnancy. A woman's lifetime risk of maternal death was one in 39. According to the UN Children's Fund (UNICEF), 55 percent of women were 18 or younger when they gave birth to their first child. There were no reports of coercive family planning practices such as female infanticide or coercive sterilization. There were no legal barriers that limit access to reproductive health services, although social and cultural barriers existed. Comprehensive information on government provisions for reproductive health services or diagnosis and treatment of sexually transmitted infections was not readily available, although the government worked closely with international partners to address this shortcoming for the future. Information on the prevention of the spread of HIV was more available than in the past.

Discrimination: Under the constitution and law, women enjoy the same rights and legal status as men, but societal discrimination against women remained a problem, particularly in rural areas. There were no effective mechanisms to enforce child support laws, and women generally bore the major responsibility for raising children. There were no known cases of official or private sector discrimination in employment or occupation, credit, pay, owning and/or managing a business, or housing. There were reports that parents, especially in more rural areas, were more likely to send boys to school than girls. Gender discrimination was more prevalent in terms of household responsibilities than in access to goods or services.

The law provides for equal pay for equal work, but women generally held low-level positions in state-run industries and in the private sector or worked in the informal sector. In an inter-ministerial effort led by the ministry of family and the protection of women, the government undertook multiple information campaigns on women's rights and domestic abuse and hosted national, provincial, and municipal workshops and training sessions during the year.

Children

Birth Registration: Citizenship is derived by birth within the country's territory or from one's parents. The government does not register all births immediately, and activists reported that many urban and rural children remained undocumented. According to UNICEF, as of the middle of this year as many as 69 percent of children under the age of five were not documented with birth certificates. The government permitted undocumented children to go to school but only up to the fourth grade. Parents could register their children under five for no fee, but prohibitive registration costs were incurred by parents with older children. In August the government announced a plan to waive registration fees for all persons, including adults, through the end of 2016; however, there were reports that officials in remote provinces continued to demand registration fees. The government continued to implement a previous plan to provide birth certificates in health clinics and maternity wards during the year.

Education: The educational infrastructure remained in disrepair. There were insufficient schools and teachers to provide universal primary education. Education is tuition-free and compulsory for documented children until the sixth grade, but students often had significant additional expenses such as books or fees paid to education officials. These fees sometimes were extraordinary payments to help with the operations and maintenance costs of running the school, costs that were not covered by the national budget. At other times, these fees were bribes paid by families to ensure their child got a place in a classroom. In cases where parents were unable to pay the fees, children were often unable to attend school.

Children of any age in an urban area were more likely to attend school than children in a rural area. Children in rural areas generally lacked access to secondary education. Even in provincial capitals, there were not enough classroom spaces for all children. According to the United Nations Educational, Scientific, and Cultural Organization, enrollment rates were higher for boys than for girls, especially at the secondary level.

Child Abuse: Child abuse was widespread. Reports of physical abuse within the family were commonplace, and local officials largely tolerated abuse. Vulnerable children, such as orphans or those without access to health care or education, were more likely to be abused by their caretakers. The 2012 Law on the Protection and Holistic Development of Children significantly improved the legal framework protecting children, but challenges remained in its implementation and enforcement.

Forced and Early Marriage: The legal age for marriage, with parental consent, is 15 years. The government did not enforce this restriction effectively, and the traditional age of marriage in lower income groups coincided with the onset of puberty. Data on the rate of marriage for boys and girls under age 18 was not available. Common-law marriage was practiced regularly.

Harmful Traditional Practices: The National Institute for Religious Affairs acknowledged that belief in and accusations of witchcraft still existed, particularly in Zaire and Uige provinces, but stated that cases of abusive practices diminished significantly due to campaigns and government directives aimed at reducing indigenous religious practices that included shamanism, animal sacrifices, and witchcraft. There were anecdotal reports of women and children being abused because of accusations they practiced witchcraft. For example, in February residents of a community in Kwanza Norte beat a young man to death because they believed he was practicing witchcraft. The assailants reportedly fled town after the attack. It was unknown if police apprehended them.

Sexual Exploitation of Children: All forms of prostitution, including child prostitution, are illegal. Police did not actively enforce laws against prostitution, and local NGOs expressed concern over child prostitution, especially in Luanda, Benguela, and Cunene provinces. Penalties for sexual exploitation of children are not specifically defined in the law.

Sexual relations between an adult and a child under the age of 12 are considered rape and carry a potential legal penalty of eight to 12 years' imprisonment. Sexual relations with a child between the ages of 12 and 17 is considered sexual abuse, with convicted offenders liable for sentences from two to eight years in prison. Limited investigative resources and an inadequate judicial system prevented prosecution of most cases. There were no known prosecutions during the year. The legal age for consensual sex is 18 years. Pornography is not prohibited by law.

The 2012 Law on the Protection and Holistic Development of Children codified the "11 Commitments to Children" campaign. The law defines priorities and coordinates the government's policies to combat all forms of abuse against children, including unlawful child labor, trafficking, and sexual exploitation.

International Child Abductions: The country is not a party to the 1980 Hague Convention on the Civil Aspects of International Child Abduction.

Anti-Semitism

There is a Jewish community of approximately 350 persons, primarily Israelis. There were no reports of anti-Semitic acts.

Trafficking in Persons

See the Department of State's *Trafficking in Persons Report* at www.state.gov/j/tip/.

Persons with Disabilities

The law prohibits discrimination against persons with disabilities, including persons with physical, sensory, intellectual, and mental disabilities, in employment, education, and access to health care or other state services, but the government did not effectively enforce these prohibitions. Article 83 of the constitution grants persons with disabilities full rights without restrictions and calls on the government to adopt national policies to prevent, treat, rehabilitate and integrate people with disabilities, to support their families, to remove obstacles to their mobility, to educate society about disability, and to encourage special learning and training opportunities for the disabled. It does not specifically mention the rights of persons with disabilities with regard to transportation, including air travel.

Persons with disabilities included more than 80,000 land-mine and other ERW victims. The NGO Handicap International estimated that, in total, up to 500,000 persons lived with disabilities. Only 30 percent of persons with disabilities were able to take advantage of state-provided services such as physical rehabilitation, schooling, training, or counseling. In 2010 the Inter-Ministerial Commission for Demining and Humanitarian Assistance began a comprehensive nationwide survey of mine victims, but as of September it had completed surveys of only six of the 18 provinces.

In 2012 the president created the national council for persons with disabilities to ensure that all disabled persons are protected from discrimination and have access to the same rights and privileges as nondisabled citizens. Persons with disabilities, however, found it difficult to access public or private facilities, and it was difficult for such persons to find employment or participate in the education system. Women with disabilities were reported to be vulnerable to sexual abuse and abandonment when pregnant. The ministry of assistance and social reinsertion sought to address problems facing persons with disabilities, including veterans with disabilities, and several government entities supported programs to assist individuals disabled by landmine incidents. During the August 2012 election, the government provided voting assistance to persons with disabilities. Persons with disabilities were allowed to select someone of their own choosing to accompany them to the voting booth to fill out the ballot and were allowed to move ahead of others waiting in line to vote.

Indigenous People

An estimated 8,000 San persons lived in small dispersed communities in Huila, Cunene, and Cuando Cubango provinces. The San are traditional hunter-gatherers who are linguistically and ethnically distinct from their Bantu fellow citizens. The constitution does not make specific reference to the rights of indigenous persons, and the ministry of justice and human rights has not established outposts near San settlements to help them register or provide them services. The San people's limited participation in political life increased slightly, and Mbakita, a local NGO advocate for the San, worked with provincial governments to increase services to San communities and improve communication between these communities and the government. The government reportedly permitted businesses and well-connected elites to take traditional land from the San, and some San were working as farmers for urban Bantus to earn a living. Those who borrowed land from Bantus lacked equipment to cultivate them, and borrowed lands can be taken back at any time. Many San have reportedly turned to begging since other options were not available.

Societal Abuses, Discrimination, and Acts of Violence Based on Sexual Orientation and Gender Identity

The law criminalizes same-sex sexual activity, although there were no reported cases of this law being enforced. A draft penal code to replace the existing code (which was adopted in 1886 and, with several amendments, was valid at year's end) was passed in 2011, but was awaiting approval by the national assembly.

Nevertheless, the draft code was used intermittently by the justice system and recognizes the right to same-sex relationships. The constitution defines marriage as between a man and a woman. NGOs reported a small underground lesbian, gay, bisexual and transgender (LGBT) community in Luanda, although an LGBT group calling itself "The Divas" held the first ever gay pride parade in the country in November. There were isolated reports of same-sex couples being harassed by their communities. There were no registered NGOs advocating for the rights of LGBT persons. There were no known reports of discrimination in employment or occupation, although a prominent transsexual musician was reportedly banned from performing on a state-run television channel because of her sexuality.

Other Societal Violence or Discrimination

Discrimination against those with HIV/AIDS is illegal, but lack of enforcement allowed employers to discriminate against persons with the condition or disease. There were no reports of violence against persons with HIV/AIDS. The government's National Institute for the Fight Against HIV/AIDS conducted HIV/AIDS awareness and prevention campaigns. Local NGOs worked to combat stigmatization and discrimination against persons living with HIV/AIDS.

Unlike in previous years, there were no official or unofficial reports of discrimination against persons with albinism. Persons with albinism reportedly were well integrated socially and culturally.

Section 7. Worker Rights

a. Freedom of Association and the Right to Collective Bargaining

The law provides for the right of private sector workers to form and join independent unions. The law allows unions to conduct their activities without government interference and grants workers, except public sector employees and oil workers, the right to strike. The law does not prohibit employer retribution against strikers, and it permits the government to force workers back to work for "breaches of worker discipline" or participation in unauthorized strikes. The law protects the right to collective bargaining, and there are no legal restrictions on collective bargaining. The law prohibits antiunion discrimination and stipulates that worker complaints be adjudicated in the labor court. Under the law employers are required to reinstate workers who have been dismissed for union activities.

The constitution grants workers the right to engage in union activities, but the government may intervene in labor disputes that affect national security, particularly strikes in the oil sector. Essential services are broadly defined. Strict bureaucratic procedures must be followed for a strike to be considered legal, and the government can deny the right to strike or obligate workers to return to work.

The government enforced applicable laws to a degree. The ministry of labor has a hotline for workers who believe their rights have been violated, and the leader of the Confederation of Free and Independent Labor Unions of Angola, an independent labor union, explained that the labor courts functioned, albeit slowly. Enforcement efforts were hampered by an insufficient number of adequately trained labor inspectors. Some companies were reportedly tipped off prior to labor inspections, making government efforts ineffective. Penalties for violations were not provided and may be insufficient to deter violations.

Freedom of association and the right to collective bargaining were not generally respected. Government approval is required to form and join unions, which were hampered by membership and legalization issues. Labor unions, independent of those run by the government, worked to increase their influence, but the ruling MPLA continued to dominate the labor movement due to historical connections between the party and labor, and the superior financial base of the country's largest labor union (which also constitutes the labor wing of the MPLA).

There were several examples during the year of workers going on strike to demand a salary increase. Government interference in some strikes was reported.

The government is the country's largest employer, and the ministry of public administration, employment, and social security centrally mandated wages with no negotiation with the unions.

b. Prohibition of Forced or Compulsory Labor

The law prohibits all forms of forced or compulsory labor.

The government did not effectively enforce the law due in part to an insufficient number of inspectors. Penalties for violations are not provided and may be insufficient to deter violations. To help bring artisanal miners into the formal economy, the governor of Malanje Province issued diamond exploration permits to 142 artisanal miners of Kunda municipality in January.

Forced labor occurred among men and women in agriculture, construction, domestic service, and artisanal diamond mining sectors, particularly in Lunda Norte and Lunda Sul. Migrant workers were subject to seizure of passports, threats, denial of food, and confinement. The government produced a training video for law enforcement and immigration officials that included a short segment on how to identify victims of trafficking, although this was not the sole objective of the film. The national institute of children (INAC) continued working to reduce the number of children traveling to agricultural areas in the country's southern regions to work on farms, mostly through community outreach about the importance of an education. Forced child labor also occurred (see section 7.c.).

See also the Department of State's *Trafficking in Persons Report* at www.state.gov/j/tip/.

c. Prohibition of Child Labor and Minimum Age for Employment

The law prohibits children under 14 from working. To obtain an employment contract, the law requires youth to submit evidence they are 14 years of age or older. Children could work from age 14 to 16 with parental permission or without parental consent if they are married, as long as work did not interfere with schooling. The ministry of labor generally effectively enforced child labor standards in the formal sector. Reports indicated, however, that employers were often tipped off before the arrival of labor inspectors, which allowed them to circumvent child labor law. Additionally, the government had difficulty monitoring the large informal sector, where most children worked.

Inspectors are authorized to conduct surprise inspections whenever they see fit. Penalties for not signing a written contract for children ages 14 and over is a fine of two to five times the median monthly salary offered by the company. Children over age 14 who are employed as part of an apprenticeship are also required to have a written contract. The penalty for not having this contract is three to six times the monthly salary of the company. For children found to be working in jobs categorized as hazardous (which is illegal under the law), the fines are five to 10 times the average monthly salary of the company. Nonpayment of any of these fines results in the accrual of additional fines.

Child labor, especially in the informal sector, remained a problem. The ministry of public administration, employment, and social security had oversight of formal work sites in all 18 provinces, but it was unknown if inspectors checked on the age of workers or conditions of work sites. If the ministry determined a business was using child labor, it transferred the case to the ministry of interior to investigate and possibly press charges. It was not known if the government fined any businesses for using child labor. The ministry of public administration, employment, and social security, along with other government agencies, and labor unions developed a national plan against child labor. This had not been implemented as of October.

In February police arrested two individuals involved in a child trafficking case. One of the two men was caught driving a truck carrying 54 children from Huila Province to tomato farms in nearby Namibe Province. The other individual gave the driver instructions on where to pick up and deliver the children. The men were in detention awaiting trial. Reactions from local communities in the area were varied, as some people considered child labor to be a valuable source of income for the family. INAC led a delegation to the provinces to speak to all interested parties, and the director of INAC remained personally engaged with her staff in the area and with local officials to eliminate child labor along this agricultural corridor.

Generally, work done by children was in the informal sector. Children engaged in economic activities such as agricultural labor on family farms and commercial plantations, fishing, brick making, charcoal production, domestic labor, and street vending. Exploitive labor practices included involvement in the sale or transport of illegal drugs, and the offloading and transport of goods in ports and across border posts. Children were reportedly forced to act as couriers in the illegal cross-border trade with Namibia. Adult criminals sometimes used children under the age of 12 for forced criminal activity, since the justice system prevents youth from being tried in court.

Street work among children was common, especially in the provinces of Luanda, Benguela, Huambo, Huila, and Kwanza Sul. Investigators found children working in the streets of Luanda, but many returned to some form of dwelling during the evening. Most of these children shined shoes, washed cars, carried water and other goods, or engaged in other informal labor, but some resorted to petty crime and begging. Commercial sexual exploitation of children occurred as well (see section 6, Children).

The ministry of interior and the ministry of justice and human rights are charged with investigating and prosecuting cases of child labor, although there were no reports of any such prosecutions during the year.

The government, through INAC, worked to create, train, and strengthen child protection networks at the provincial and municipal levels in all 18 provinces. The networks reported cases in which they successfully identified and removed children from exploitative work situations, but no mechanism existed to track cases or provide statistics. The government also dedicated resources to the expansion of educational and livelihood opportunities for children and their families.

Also see the Department of Labor's *Findings on the Worst Forms of Child Labor* at www.dol.gov/ilab/programs/ocft/tda.htm.

d. Acceptable Conditions of Work

The minimum wage was 10,900 kwanzas ($115) per month for all formal sectors. Workers in informal sectors, such as street vendors, subsistence agriculture, and domestic service, are not covered by the minimum wage law. The country had not established a poverty income level; however, the United Nations Development Program estimated the poverty level to be 165 kwanzas ($1.70) per day or 4,950 kwanzas($52) per month.

The standard workweek is 40 hours, with a maximum allowance per week of 44 hours without paying overtime, and with at least one unbroken period of 24 hours of rest per week. When an employee works shift work or a variable weekly schedule they can work up to 54 hours per week before earning overtime. In the formal sector, there is a prohibition on excessive compulsory overtime, defined as more than two hours a day, 40 hours a month, or 200 hours a year. The law also provides for paid annual holidays. The government sets occupational health and safety standards. Workers have the right to remove themselves from situations that endanger health or safety without jeopardy to their employment.

Most wage earners held second jobs or depended on the agricultural or other informal sectors to augment their incomes. The majority of citizens derived their income from the informal sector or subsistence agriculture and therefore fell outside of government protection regarding working conditions. Foreign workers also were not generally covered by government protections.

The minimum wage law was effectively enforced only in the formal sector. Informal sector workers were not covered by wage or occupational safety standards in most cases. The workweek standards were not enforced unless employees lodged a formal complaint with the ministry of public administration, employment, and social security.

The Ministry Of Labor's inspector general did not effectively enforce standards for acceptable work conditions. The government had 187 inspectors--53 senior inspectors, 41 technical inspectors, and 93 junior inspectors. Upon starting work, the inspectors were given a 120-hour training course, and training for requalification and to qualify to inspect technical labor areas also existed. Inspections occurred, although rulings on labor violations found by inspectors were not effectively enforced. Specific information on penalties for violations was not provided; however, fines incurred were generally insufficient to deter infractions. Despite the law, workers were unable to remove themselves from unsafe working conditions without jeopardizing their employment. According to independent labor leaders, most workers were reluctant to complain about poor working conditions, even if they were hazardous.

Information on the number of workplace fatalities or major industrial accidents was not available.